OET UPDAT PREP PLUS FOR DOCTORS

DETAILED GUIDE FOR WRITING SPEAKING & LISTENING

JAYDEN LACHLAN

CONTENTS

INTRODUCTION TO OET WRITING SUB-TEST

The Writing sub-test takes 45 minutes and is profession-specific. There is one task set for each profession based on a typical workplace situation and the demands of the profession. The task is to write a letter, usually a referral letter. Sometimes a different type of letter is required: e.g. a letter of transfer or discharge, or a letter to advise or inform a patient, carer, or group. There is a five minutes of reading time given at the start of the Writing sub-test. Make use of this time to understand the task and the case notes and to plan your response. The tasks given in the Writing sub-test are designed in such a way that the remaining 40 minutes is enough for you to write a response of the required length and to check over what you have written. Remember that you can always consult the task and the case notes at any point during the 40 minutes allocated for writing, not just during the reading time.

Usually, the writing task will provide you with:
- The recipient's name
- The recipient's profession or position
- The recipient's place of work and address
- A reference to what type of letter you must write, e.g.: referral.

You can also see or infer from the task whether the recipient knows the patient or whether you are introducing the patient to the recipient for the first time. Learn to adapt your written communication according to the different scenarios and keeping mind the reader. For this, you have to pay attention to finding the relevant information in the case notes given in the question. You should address the intended reader of the letter using the title and address details specified in the task instructions.

Write the letter only for the recipient, keeping the recipient's needs in mind at all times. Knowing this information is critical for case note selection. The case notes are not written in perfect sentences and so you will have to interpret the case notes without any confusion. Because, if you misinterpret the case notes, it may result in letter with incorrect information. You should pay close attention while interpreting the category or sub-headings in the case notes, short ungrammatical phrases, symbols such as downward and upward arrows and abbreviations.

While reading and correctly interpreting the case notes, you will also have to think more carefully about the relevance of case note. Keeping in mind that your letter should only be between 180 and 200 words, you should not include all of the case notes. Selecting case notes is very challenging because while some case notes will clearly be relevant and irrelevant, others will be semi-relevant. You have to make decisions about which case notes to include and which case notes to ignore based on the task, to whom you are writing and why you are writing the letter. This is why practice is so important: by practicing the OET writing sub-test, you will develop an understanding of how many case notes you should include in order to write an appropriate length. You do not want to write a letter on test day that is well below or well above the word count.

Avoid repeating everything from the case notes or a chronological account. Always keep in mind that it is more important to produce a letter that is appropriate for the situation given in the task. Therefore, you should select and organize the information in a way that informs the reader appropriately and effectively. Always try to show your knowledge of workplace language which occurs frequently in health professional contexts. For that, you should regularly review common workplace expressions to make sure you can produce them appropriately and accurately while writing letter.

Always read and thoroughly understand the question to organize and prioritize the important points from the case notes effectively in your letter. Always answer yourself these three questions before you start writing the letter.

1. *Who is the intended reader?*
2. *What are the main things I want the reader to do?*
3. *What does the reader need to know?*

After selecting the relevant case notes, you have to organize the short hand case notes given in the question into paragraphs in a logical and coherent way after transforming them into accurate sentences. So, it is always wise to make rough sketch of the structures of paragraphs before your begin writing.

In the introductory sentence or paragraph, you should include the reason why you are writing the letter and the chief medical issue. You should always place the important information at the beginning of the letter, rather than burying it deep in the letter.

Always organize information within a paragraph wisely, so that it contains only related information structured coherently to make it clear to the reader what the paragraph is about in a logical order. A paragraph should be never made up with mixed information; as it can be turned out to be very confusing.

LAYOUT OF THE LETTER

There are a number of different formats, which are accepted by health professionals in different local contexts. Therefore, there is no single particular format that you have to use in the OET Writing sub-test. However, it is very important that your letter is clearly laid out and appropriate for the particular task.

The standard and widely used layout of the letter:

The title and full name of the recipient	Ms Amanda Roxby
Position or Profession of the recipient	Senior Nurse
Name of the Hospital/Clinic	Old Hill Community Nursing Home
Address of the Hospital/Clinic	108 Green Park, Old Hill
Date of your exam (Today's date)	Day/Month/Year
Re: Name of the patient, age	Re: Darwin Kilmer, aged 72 years
Salutation	Dear Ms Roxby,
Introduction	_____
First Paragraph	_____
Second Paragraph	_____
Third Paragraph, if necessary.	_____
Closing phrase	If you have any queries, please do not hesitate to contact me.
Sign off	Yours sincerely,
Your profession	Doctor.

After you finish writing, re-read what you have written from the target reader's point of view. Ask yourself whether it is clear what you have to do. If it is not clear, check to see that you have included everything relevant from the case notes. You should also check your written work in the test to correct and verify the unnecessary errors that you failed to notice while writing. It is better to prepare a mental checklist of types of error that you happen to make very often like spelling errors, punctuation or subject-verb agreement; so, always proofread your letter specifically for those errors.

PARALLEL STRUCTURES & BALANCED SENTENCES

The information in the case notes will be in note form and does not follow any conventional grammatical rules. However, when this information is transformed into complete sentences in a letter, it is very important to follow standard conventions of English grammar and sentence structure. This can be achieved by making sure that verbs, adjectives, nouns, prepositions, phrases and clauses are parallel. Parallel structures within a sentence are joined with coordinating conjunctions such as and/or as well as with commas. Here are some examples:

With active verbs

- *She is now worried about her condition because she **is** overweight, **lacks** exercise and **smokes** regularly.*

With passive verbs

- *During hospitalization, IV fluids **were commenced** and a transdermal patch **was used** for her pain.*

With nouns & noun phrases

- *She is now worried about her condition because of her **increased weight**, **lack of exercise** and **her habit of smoking.***

- *She will require information about **how and when to take her medication, how to stop smoking** and **the necessity of doing regular exercise.***

With gerunds

- *In order to handle the above-mentioned effects be cautious when **driving** a car, **operating** machinery or **performing** any hazardous activities especially after **taking** your regular dose.*

With prepositions

- *Threadworms resemble pieces of 1.5 cm cotton thread, which is normally detectable **at** the surface of the feces or **around** the anus at night.*

With verbs in the conclusion

- *I **am** worried about Mr. Zane and **would** appreciate your urgent assessment and treatments as you think appropriate.*

NB: The important point to remember is that the structures must be balanced.

STARTERS & PHRASES FOR WRITING LETTER

Opening Clause

Referral letter

Thank you for (urgently) **seeing** (the above patient/ Mr. Zane),
/**a 49 year-old** (worker, profession) **with** (medical condition) **for further** (management) **and possible** (operation).
/**who is currently**
/**in this hospital recovering from/ suffering from** (medical condition)
/**bedridden/immobile with possible** (medical condition) **following** (type of activity that led to the medical condition) **on** (date).

Or,

I am writing to refer/ I am pleased to refer (the above patient/ Mr. Zane) **aged 49 and** married **with** three children of school age.

Reason for Referral

(Mr. Zane) **presented to me** (today) **with signs of a** (possible) (medical condition)
/**at my clinic complaining of** (symptom).
/**to emergency.**

(Mr. Zane) **initially presented with** (medical condition) **for which he was treated with** (medication).

He has been suffering his first episode of (medical condition).

He was admitted to this hospital on
/**for a fracture of his/her** (name of the bone).

/suffering from (medical condition).

/with signs for early (medical condition).

Admission letter

(Mr. Zane/ The patient) **was admitted to (your facility)/ this hospital/ clinic on (date) for**

   /further (type of [e.g.: neurological]) **assessment and possible treatment of** (medical condition).

   /operation of (medical condition).

   /management of (medical condition).

   /for a fracture of his/her (name of the bone).

   /for post fracture rehabilitation.

Advice letter

(Further to our earlier conversation, I am reporting you about)/ (I am writing to follow up our conversation earlier today about) (the intro [e.g.: your son's management plan]).

Provisional Diagnosis *(not yet diagnosed)*

My provisional diagnosis is (medical condition), **possibly related to** (cause).

He/ She are diagnosed with (medical condition).

The complaints may result from (medical condition) **caused by** (cause).

I believe he/she has (medical condition).

I believe that the cause of his complaints is (medical condition) **and is at risk of developing** (...).

Investigation Diagnosis

The (test) **indicated possible** (medical condition)

The (organ) **function tests showed possible** (medical condition).

The X-ray detected (medical condition).

Present Illness

He/ She first attended my clinic for a check-up complaining of / suffering from (symptom).
with symptoms of (medical condition)

On his/her first visit to me on (date) **he was / has been suffering** (symptom).

On (date) **Mr. Zane presented at my clinic/ the hospital complaining of** (symptom) **for the previous (time period) which was not responding to** (medication).

His/ Her complaints set in (time period) **earlier and were related to** (activity performed).

Symptoms

Apart from this,	he/she			
In addition,		experienced	a new episode of	(symptom)
Moreover,		reported	no further	
Otherwise,		noticed	progressively worsening	
At times,				
Occasionally,				

He/ She (initially) **had** (symptom), **but has had none since that time until** (now / [time period] ago).

He/ She reported no history of (symptom).

Past History

(Using past tense)

[**He/ She reported**]/ [**There has been no history of**] (medical condition/ being overweight).

He/ She has not suffered from (medical condition) **or other significant illness/injuries before** (accident/ incident).

(Using present tense)

He/ She has a (time period) **history of** (medical condition)

He/ She has a history of (medical condition) **well controlled by** (medication).

His/ Her (medical) **history includes** (specifics) **for which he/she is given /treated with** (medication).

Current Medication

Abbreviations:

stat (Latin: statim) – immediately

BD – twice times   **t.d.s. /t.i.d.** – thrice   **q.d.s. /q.i.d.** – four

p.c. – after food   **nocte** – at night

s.l. – sublingual   **s.c.** – subcutaneous

His/ Her current medications include/ are (the list).

He/ She also uses (medication) **for** (purpose).

No effect/effect

The pain

     /has (not) **responded to** (medication).

     /was (not) **relieved by** (medication).

     /was persistent.

     /resistant to (medication).

His/ Her complaint usually settles with (medication).

Side effect

However, the medication caused significant {side effect).

Treatment

Prescription

He was treated here with (prescription).

Combination Treatment

He was given (first/ more important treatment)
>**/followed by** (second/ less important treatment).
>**/in addition to** (second/ less important treatment).
>**/combined with** (second/ less important treatment).
>**/and advised on** (advice).

I prescribed (first/ more important treatment)
>**/combined with** (second/ less important treatment).
>**/in addition to** (second/ less important treatment).

Effect

Initially his response to (treatment) **was good, but unfortunately, his/ her pain flared up. Therefore,**
>**/I commenced him on** (the change made).
>**/I changed him on** (the change made).

Dose

After persistently elevated (readings around x units), **he/ she was commenced/started on** (medication), **this has recently been increased to** (dose).

Operation

A/ An (operation) **was performed.**

He/ She underwent/ had (a/an operation) **and recovered well/ will be discharged today.**

Recovery

He/ She has been able to (activity) **with assistance.**

Since the operation, his/her wounds have healed and sutures have been removed.

His/ Her postoperative recovery was successful/ uncomplicated/ uneventful /normal.

Subsequently, / In the following days, he/she recovered by taking (medication) **for** (time period). /after (time period) **treatment with** (medication).

Complications

While here, he/she	**has (extreme) difficulty**	**using a walking frame / the crutches.**
		to walk./ to walk with extreme difficulty.
	has been able	**to have shower with assistance.**

His/ Her (medical condition) **has worsened while here.**

His/ Her general condition has deteriorated.

Examination

	neurological		he/she scored (score) **on a** (test).
On	physical	examination	no abnormalities were found.
	cardiovascular		he/she was (condition) **with normal vital signs.**

The examination was unremarkable/ normal.

The examination revealed elevated (findings)/**no abnormalities.**

(Findings) **were noted on** (name of) **examination.**

Otherwise, examination was normal.

Readings

The (name of tests)

    /**showed** (no) **pathological findings/ significant abnormalities.**

    /**were consistent with** (medical condition).

Technical Investigations

Tests including/ The tests taken here on Mr. Zane revealed/ indicated no significant abnormalities.

Tests for/on Mr. Zane were done and showed (findings).
I had test for Mr. Zane done which showed (findings).
I ordered the following test for Mr. Zane, which showed (findings).

Results

All tests in summary

> **indicate pathological findings consistent with** (medical condition).
> **confirm my provisional diagnosis of** (medical condition).

(Tests) showed/ confirmed significant (medical condition).
(Tests) showed possible (medical condition).
The (test) **at that time appeared** (unremarkable/ normal).

Review

On review today, Mr. Zane reports no further episodes of (symptom).

On review, investigations showed (medical condition).

Concerns

	was anxious	
	showed concerns	**that she may have** (medical condition), **about which I have reassured her.**
He/ She		
	worried	

He/ She is most concerned of (concern).

He/ She is a widower/widow and has managed alone until now.

	receives	support from	
He/ She	needs	assistance	**to manage** (concern)
	requires		

Advice

He/ She was advised to/ on (advice) **and return in** (time period).

Mr. Zane was given advice on (advice).

I advised him/her that he/she might need to re-present to hospital for admission

>   **/if he/she gets any worse.**

>   **/or if he/she is not getting better in** (time period).

To avoid future episodes, he/ she needs (advice).

Request/ Future Management

I would appreciate your further assessment and management/treatment

>   **/regarding his/ her** (medical condition).

>   **/of the possibility of** (medical condition).

>   **/of the suspected/potential** (medical condition).

I would appreciate/ be grateful

>   / (for) **your opinion regarding his/her future management.**

>   **/if you could please assess this patient.**

>   **/if you could see Mr. Zane fairly soon for further management.**

>   **/if you could arrange an appointment with**

>>   **/a physiotherapist.**

>>   **/an occupational therapist.**

>>   **/a social worker.**

I would be interested if he/she would be a suitable candidate for (medical procedure).

I would appreciate if you could keep me informed about his/her further management.

OET SPEAKING ASSESSMENT CRITERIA

Your performance on the Writing sub-test is marked independently by a minimum of two trained Assessors. Neither Assessor knows what scores the other has given you, or what scores you have achieved on any of the other sub-tests. Your performance is scored against five criteria and receives a band score for each criterion:

1. Overall Task Fulfillment

This criterion assesses the candidate's performance on all the analytical criteria; in addition to the assessor's general view of the effectiveness of the candidate's writing sample.

2. Appropriateness of Language

This criterion assesses accurate use of appropriate vocabulary and expression, as well as organization and style of the letter. This assessment also considers control of genre and the level of formality that is polite and relatively formal. The response should be logically organized in a formulaic sequence appropriate to both task and professional context.

3. Comprehension of Stimulus

This criterion assesses the extent to which the candidate understands the stimulus notes and task requirements. It focuses on the selection and transformation of relevant material from the notes and is thus concerned with adequacy of content (coverage of main points) and accuracy of interpretation of the task instructions.

4. Linguistic Features (Grammar and Cohesion)

This criterion assesses the extent to which the response demonstrates control of grammatical elements and cohesive devices to express and connect information clearly. Cohesion also refers to the use of appropriate pronouns, conjunctions and connectives, including the absence of redundancy and repetition.

5. Presentation Features (Spelling, Punctuation and Layout)

This criterion assesses the extent to which the candidate demonstrates control of spelling and conventions of punctuation to produce writing that reads clearly and without strain. This criterion also assesses the conventional layout of the letter, the inclusion of the addressee's name and address, and the opening and closing salutations.

Dos

- Summarize all the information from the case notes into sections such as treatment given and obvious trends, medication, medical history. This will be both easier to write and read as well as avoiding repetition.

- Try to write somewhere between 180 and 200 words for the body of the letter.

- Omit information, which is not directly relevant to your task. This is a big trap for many candidates in that they try to write down all the information from the task sheet.

- Provide a simple clear summary of the condition so that a layperson could understand.

- Use articles such as a/the before countable nouns as this is a requirement of formal writing.

- Use synonyms so that you can express the information from the case notes in different ways.

- Spend time reading the case notes and grouping information which are related such as medication, persistent high blood pressure etc etc.

- Allow 5 minutes at the end of the test to proof read your work and fix up any mistakes.

Don'ts

- Follow a strict chronological order as your letter may become too long, difficult to read and will not focus on the main problem and related factors.

- Write over 220 words as it may affect your overall result. You being tested on your ability to write a clear concise letter, not a long letter.

- Do not write under 160 words, as there may not be sufficient range language to get a B grade.

- Try to put all the information from the case notes into the letter. Your letter will be too long and also poorly organized and difficult to read.

- Use medical jargon.

- Forget that case notes are written in short form, so they do not follow standard grammatical rules. For example, it is common to omit articles.

- Copy directly from the case notes without any changes. You are expected to put the information into your own words.

- Start writing without planning your letter. You should allow 10 to 15 minutes reading case notes and planning the letter.

- Submit the letter without checking for basic mistakes such as grammar/spelling.

Abbreviations in the Letter

Abbreviations that are commonly accepted in the candidate's profession and clear to the assessors can be used in the writing sub-test. If your target reader is a health professional, a number of commonly used abbreviations are likely to be acceptable. However, if you are writing to somebody from a non-health professional background, full word-forms may be more preferable. For example, BMI for body mass index, or units of measurement such as mg, whereas you should write OPG as orthopantamogram, PR as pulse rate and hx as history. Therefore, you should always consider who the intended reader is, while using abbreviations. OET Assessors do not refer to any specific lists of abbreviations and there is no recommended dictionary or handbook of abbreviations.

Writing sub-test
Medicine
Sample Test 1

Please print in BLOCK LETTERS

Candidate number ☐☐☐ – ☐☐☐ – ☐☐☐

Family name _____

Other name(s) _____

City _____

Date of test _____

Candidate's signature _____

YOU MUST NOT REMOVE OET MATERIAL FROM THE TEST ROOM

OCCUPATIONAL ENGLISH TEST

WRITING SUB-TEST: MEDICINE

TIME ALLOWED: **READING TIME:**   **5 MINUTES**

                                WRITING TIME: **40 MINUTES**

Read the case notes and complete the writing task, which follows.

Notes:

Patient Details:

Mae Rupert

Female

30 year old, professor.

Patient in your clinic for 8 years

Has two children, 3 years old and 11 months old.

Both pregnancies and deliveries were normal.

Husband, 33 yr old, manager of a travel agency.

Living with husband's parents.

Has a F/H of schizophrenia, symptoms controlled by Risperidone

Smoking-nil, Alcohol- nil

Use of recreational drugs – nil

09/01

Subjective

c/o poor health, tiredness

low grade temperature

unmotivated at work

not enjoying her work.

No stress, loss of appetite or weight.

Objective

Appearance- nearly normal

Mood – not depressed

BP- 120/80

Pulse- 80/min

Ab, CVS, RS, CNS- normal

Management

Advised to relax, start regular exercise, and maintain a temperature chart.

If not happy, follow up visit required.

20/01
Subjective

Previous symptoms – no change

Has poor concentration and attention to job activities

finding living with husband's parents difficult.

Says her mother-in-law thinks she is lazy and is turning her husband against her.

Too tired to do much with her children, mother-in-law takes over.

Feels anxiety, poor sleep, and frequent headaches.

Objective

Mood- mildly depressed

Little eye contact

Speech- normal

Physical examination normal

Tentative diagnosis

Early depression or schizophrenia

Management plan

Relaxation therapy, counseling

Need to talk to the husband at next visit

Prescribed Diazepam 10 mg/nocte and paracetamol as required

Review in 2/52

10/02

Subjective

Accompanied by husband and he said that she tries to avoid eye contact with other people

reduced speech output

Impaired planning

Some visual hallucinations and delusions for 5 days

Objective

Mood – depressed

Little eye contact

Speech – disorganized

Behavior- bizarre BP 120/80

Pulse- 80

Ab, CVS, RS, CNS- normal

Probable diagnosis

Schizophrenia and associated disorders

Management plan

Refer to psychiatrist for assessment and further management.

Writing task:

Using the information in the case notes, write a referral letter to Psychiatrist, Dr Carol Pascal, 324 Morgan Rd, Mt Herman 4782.

In your answer:

- expand the relevant notes into complete sentences

- do not use note form

- use letter format

The body of the letter should be approximately 180-200 words.

Writing sub-test
Medicine
Sample Test 2

Please print in BLOCK LETTERS

Candidate number ☐☐☐ – ☐☐☐ – ☐☐☐

Family name _____

Other name(s) _____

City _____

Date of test _____

Candidate's signature _____

YOU MUST NOT REMOVE OET MATERIAL FROM THE TEST ROOM

OCCUPATIONAL ENGLISH TEST

WRITING SUB-TEST: MEDICINE

TIME ALLOWED: **READING TIME:**   **5 MINUTES**

                      WRITING TIME: **40 MINUTES**

Read the case notes and complete the writing task, which follows.

Patient Details:

John Williams, 56 year old
Regular patient in your General Practice

20.04
Subjective

Wants regular check up, has noticed small swelling in right groin.
Hypertension diagnosed 7 years ago
Non-smoker
Regularly drinks 2 – 4 glasses of wine nightly and 1 - 2 glasses of scotch at weekend.
Widower living on his own, likes cooking and says he eats well.
Current medication noten 50 mg daily, ½ aspirin daily, normison 10 mg nightly when required, fifty plus multivitamin 1 daily, allergic reaction to penicillin.

Objective

BP 155/85 P 80 regular
Cardiovascular and respiratory examination normal
Urinalysis normal
Slight swelling in right groin consistent with inguinal hernia.

Plan

Advised reduction of alcohol to two glasses maximum daily and at least one alcohol free day a week.
Discussed options regarding hernia.
Patient wants to avoid surgery.
Advised to avoid any heavy lifting and review BP and hernia in 2 months

05.05
Subjective

Had problem lifting heavy wheelbarrow while gardening.
Has a regular dull ache in right groin
Noticed swelling has increased.
Has reduced alcohol intake as suggested.

Objective

BP 140/80 P 70 regular
Marked increase in swelling in right groin and small swelling in left groin.

Assessment

Bilateral inguinal hernia
Advise patient you want to refer him to a surgeon.
He agrees but says he wants a local anesthetic.
As a friend advised him, he will have less after effects than with general anesthetic.

Writing task:

Write a letter to Dr Gladwin Beckett, 37 Park St, Perth explaining the patient's current condition.

.

In your answer:

• expand the relevant notes into complete sentences

• do not use note form

• use letter format

The body of the letter should be approximately 180-200 words.

Writing sub-test
Medicine
Sample Test 3

Please print in BLOCK LETTERS

Candidate number ☐☐☐ – ☐☐☐ – ☐☐☐

Family name _____

Other name(s) _____

City _____

Date of test _____

Candidate's signature _____

YOU MUST NOT REMOVE OET MATERIAL FROM THE TEST ROOM

OCCUPATIONAL ENGLISH TEST

WRITING SUB-TEST: **MEDICINE**

TIME ALLOWED: **READING TIME:**   **5 MINUTES**

                    WRITING TIME: **40 MINUTES**

Read the case notes and complete the writing task, which follows.

Notes:

Patient Details:

Reagan Gilchrist, 46 year old

Regular patient in your General Practice

18.07

Subjective

Regular check up

Family man, wife, three sons aged 7, 5 and 3

Parents alive - father age 73 diagnosed with prostate cancer.

Mother age 69 hypertension diagnosed.

Smokes 18 cigarettes per day –trying to give up

Works long hours – no regular exercise

Light drinker 3 – 4 beers a week

Objective

BP 165/90 P 80 regular

Cardiovascular and respiratory examination normal

Height 172 cm

Weight 86 kg

Urinalysis normal

Plan

Advice regarding weight loss,

smoking cessation

Review BP in 1 month

Request PSA test before next visit

29.08

Subjective

Reduced smoking to 8 per day

Attends gym twice a week,

Weight 76 kg

Complains of discomfort urinating

Objective

BP 145/80 P 76

DRE hardening and enlargement of prostate

PSA reading 10

Plan

Review BP, smoking reduction in 2 months

Refer to urologist – possible biopsy prostate

Writing task:

Using the information given in the case notes, write a referral letter to Dr Mitchell Drew (Urologist), 225 Baker St, Adelaide 3004.

In your answer:

- expand the relevant notes into complete sentences

- do not use note form

- use letter format

The body of the letter should be approximately 180-200 words.

Writing sub-test
Medicine
Sample Test 4

Please print in BLOCK LETTERS

Candidate number ☐☐☐ – ☐☐☐ – ☐☐☐

Family name _____

Other name(s) _____

City _____

Date of test _____

Candidate's signature _____

YOU MUST NOT REMOVE OET MATERIAL FROM THE TEST ROOM

OCCUPATIONAL ENGLISH TEST

WRITING SUB-TEST: MEDICINE

TIME ALLOWED: **READING TIME:**   **5 MINUTES**

                                  WRITING TIME: **40 MINUTES**

Read the case notes and complete the writing task, which follows.

Notes:

Patient Details

Lindsay McCarthy, 50 years old

Gender: Female

Regular patient in your General Practice.

24.01

Subjective

Wants general check up,

Single, lives with and takes care of elderly mother.

Father died bowel cancer aged 52.

Had colonoscopy 2 years ago. Clear

Does not smoke or drink

Objective

BP 160/90 PR 70 regular Ht 152 cm

Wt 68 kg

On no medication.

No known allergies.

Assessment

Overweight.

Advised on exercise & weight reduction.

Borderline hypertension.

Review in 2 months

25.03
Subjective

Feeling better in part due to weight loss

Objective

BP 140/85

PR 70 regular

Ht 152 cm, Wt 60 kg

Assessment

Making good progress with weight.

Blood pressure within normal range

07.06
Subjective

Saw blood in the toilet bowl on two occasions after bowel motions.

Depressed and very anxious.

Believes she has bowel cancer.

Trouble sleeping.

Objective

BP 180/95 P 88 regular

Ht 152 cm Wt 50 kg

Cardiovascular and respiratory examination normal.

Rectal examination shows no obvious abnormalities.

Assessment

Need to investigate for bowel cancer

Refer to gastroenterologist for assessment /colonoscopy.

Prescribe 15 gram Alepam 1 tablet before bed.

Advise patient this is temporary measure to ease current anxiety/sleeplessness.

Review after BP appointment with gastroenterologist

Writing task:

Write a referral letter to Dr Patrick Simmons, 76 Park Ave, Sydney, 5023 requesting his opinion.

In your answer:

- expand the relevant notes into complete sentences

- do not use note form

- use letter format

The body of the letter should be approximately 180-200 words.

Writing sub-test
Medicine
Sample Test 5

Please print in BLOCK LETTERS

Candidate number   ☐☐☐ – ☐☐☐ – ☐☐☐

Family name   _____

Other name(s)   _____

City   _____

Date of test   _____

Candidate's signature   _____

YOU MUST NOT REMOVE OET MATERIAL FROM THE TEST ROOM

OCCUPATIONAL ENGLISH TEST

WRITING SUB-TEST: MEDICINE

TIME ALLOWED: **READING TIME:**   **5 MINUTES**

WRITING TIME: **40 MINUTES**

Read the case notes and complete the writing task, which follows.

Notes:

Patient Details:

Mr David Taylor, 38 years old

Married, 3 children

Landscape Gardener

Runs own business.

No personal injury insurance

Active, enjoys sports

Drinks 1-2 beers a day. More on weekends.

Smokes 20-30 cigarettes/day

P.M.H- Left Inguinal Hernia Operation

12/08

Subjective

C/o left knee joint pain and swelling, difficulty in strengthening the leg.

Has history of twisting L/K joint 6 months ago in a game of tennis.

At that time, the joint was painful, swollen, and responded to pain killers.

Finds injury is inhibiting his ability to work productively.

Worried as needs regular income to support family and home repayments.

Objective

Has limp, slightly swollen L/K joint, tender spot on medial aspect of the joint and no effusion.

Temperature- normal BP 120/80

Pulse rate -78/min Investigation - X ray knee joint

Management

Voltarin 50 mg bid for 1/52

Advise to reduce smoking

Review if no improvement.

25/8

Subjective

Had experienced intermittent attacks of pain and swelling of the L/K joint

No fever

Unable to complete all aspects of his work and as a result income reduced

Reduced smoking 15/day

Objective

Swelling + No effusion

Tender on the inner-aspect of the L/K joint Flexion, extension – normal

Impaired range of power - passive & active

Diagnosis? Injury of medial cartilage Investigation – ordered MRI

Management

Voltarin 50 mg bid for 1 week

Review after 1 week with investigations

07/11

Subjective

Limp still present

Patient anxious as has been unable to maintain full time work.

Desperate to resolve the problem

Weight increase of 5 kg

Objective

Pain decreased, swelling – no change

No new complications

MRI report – damaged medial cartilage

Management Plan

Refer to an orthopedic surgeon to remove damaged cartilage in order to prevent future osteoporosis.

Writing task:

Using the information in the case notes, write referral letter to Orthopedic Surgeon, Dr James Brown, 1238 Gympie Road, Chermside, 4352.

In your answer:

- expand the relevant notes into complete sentences

- do not use note form

- use letter format

The body of the letter should be approximately 180-200 words.

OCCUPATIONAL ENGLISH TEST

Sample Test 1

WRITING SUB-TEST: MEDICINE

SAMPLE RESPONSE: LETTER

Dr Carol Pascal

 324 Morgan Rd

Mt Herman 4782

(Today's Date)

Re: Mae Rupert

Dear Dr Pascal

I am writing to refer Mrs. Rupert, a 30-year-old married woman, who is presenting with symptoms suggestive of schizophrenia.

Mrs. Rupert has been a patient at my clinic for the last 8 years and has a family history of schizophrenia. She is a teacher with two children, aged 4 years and 10 months, and lives with her husband's parents.

She first presented at my clinic on January 9 complaining of tiredness, a lack of motivation at work and a low-grade fever. On review after ten days, she did not show any improvement. She displayed symptoms of paranoia and was suffering from poor sleep, anxiety and frequent headaches. In addition, she was mildly depressed with little eye contact. Relaxation therapy and counseling were started and Diazepam 10 mg at night was prescribed based on my provisional diagnosis of early depression or schizophrenia.

She presented today accompanied by her husband in a depressed state, showing little eye contact, bizarre behavior and disorganized speech. Despite my management, her symptoms have continued to worsen with a 5-day history of reduced speech output, impaired planning ability as well as some visual hallucinations and delusions.

In view of the above, I would appreciate your attention to this patient.

Yours sincerely

Doctor

OCCUPATIONAL ENGLISH TEST

Sample Test 2

WRITING SUB-TEST: MEDICINE

SAMPLE RESPONSE: LETTER

Dr Gladwin Beckett

37 Park St

Perth

(Today's Date)

Re: Mr. John Williams, 56 year old

Dear Dr Beckett,

I am referring this patient, a widower, who is presenting with symptoms consistent with a bilateral inguinal hernia. He has been suffering from hypertension for 7 years for which he takes Noten, Aspirin and multivitamins. He is allergic to penicillin.

Initially, Mr. Williams presented to me on April 20th for a regular check up. On examination, he had a mild swelling of the right groin, his blood pressure was 155/85 and pulse was 80 beats per minute, otherwise his condition was normal. He was diagnosed as having an inguinal hernia. I discussed the possibility of surgery; however, he indicated he did not want an operation. Therefore, I advised that he avoid heavy lifting and reduce alcohol consumption. A review consultation was scheduled for two months later.

Today, he returned complaining that his right groin had increased in size with a regular dull ache possibly due to lifting a heavy wheelbarrow. The examination revealed a considerable increase in swelling in the right groin as well as a mild swelling of the left groin.

Based on my provisional diagnosis of a bilateral inguinal hernia, I would like to refer him for surgery as early as possible. Please note that he wishes to have the surgery under local anesthesia.

Yours sincerely

Doctor

OCCUPATIONAL ENGLISH TEST

Sample Test 3

WRITING SUB-TEST: MEDICINE

SAMPLE RESPONSE: LETTER

Dr Mitchell Brooker

225 Baker St

Adelaide 3004

(Today's Date)

Re: Mr. Reagan Gilchrist

Dear Dr Brooker,

I am writing to refer this patient, a 46 year old married man with three sons aged 3, 5 and 7, who requires screening for prostate cancer.

Initial examination on July 18th revealed a strong family history of related illness as elderly father was diagnosed with prostate cancer and mother was diagnosed as hypertensive. Mr. Gilchrist is a smoker and light drinker. He works long hours and does not do any regular exercise. His blood pressure was initially 165/90 mm hg and pulse was 80 and regular. He is 172 cm tall and his weight, at that time, was 86 kg. He was advised to reduce weight and stop smoking and a prostate specific antigen test was requested. There were no other remarkable findings.

When he came for the next visit on August 29th, Mr. Gilchrist had reduced smoking from 18 to 8 cigarettes per day and was attending gym twice a week. He had lost 10 kg of weight. His blood pressure was improved at 165/90. However, digital rectal examination revealed an enlarged prostate and the PSA reading was 10.

In view of the above signs and symptoms, I believe he needs further investigations including a prostate biopsy and surgical management. I would appreciate your urgent attention for his condition.

Yours sincerely

Doctor

OCCUPATIONAL ENGLISH TEST

Sample Test 4

WRITING SUB-TEST: MEDICINE

SAMPLE RESPONSE: LETTER

Dr Patrick Simmons

76 Park Ave

Sydney 5023

(Today's Date)

Re: Lindsay McCarthy, 50 years old

Dear Dr Simmons,

Thank you for seeing my patient, Lindsay McCarthy, who has been very concerned about blood in her stools. She has seen blood in the toilet bowl on two occasions after bowel motion. She is very anxious and as well as that depressed because her father died of bowel cancer and she feels she may have the same condition.

Lindsay has otherwise been quite healthy. She does not drink or smoke and is not taking any medication. She was slightly overweight five months ago with borderline high blood pressure. At that time, I advised her to lose weight, which she did successfully. Two months later, her weight had dropped from 68 kg to 60 kg and blood pressure was back within normal range.

On presentation today, she was distressed because she believes she has bowel cancer. She has had trouble sleeping and her weight has reduced a further 10 kg. The rectal examination did not show any abnormalities. Her blood pressure was slightly elevated at 180/95 but her cardiovascular and respiratory examination was unremarkable. Alepam, one before bed, was prescribed to control the anxiety and sleeplessness.

I would appreciate it if you could perform a gastroenterology assessment.

Yours sincerely

Doctor

OCCUPATIONAL ENGLISH TEST

Sample Test 5

WRITING SUB-TEST: MEDICINE

SAMPLE RESPONSE: LETTER

Dr James Brown

1238 Gympie Rd

Chermside, 4352

(Today's Date)

Re: David Taylor

Dear Dr Brown,

Thank you for seeing this patient, a 38-year-old male who has a damaged cartilage in the left knee joint. He is self-employed as a landscape gardener, and is married with three children.

Mr. Taylor first presented on August 12th complaining of pain and swelling in the left knee joint associated with difficulty in strengthening the joint. He initially twisted this joint in a game of tennis 6 months previously, experiencing pain and swelling, which had responded to painkillers. Examination revealed a slightly swollen joint and there was a tender spot in the medial aspect of the joint. Voltarin 50 mg twice daily was prescribed.

Despite this treatment, he developed intermittent pain and swelling of the joint. The x-ray showed no evidence of osteoarthritis. However, the range and power including passive and active movements was impaired. An MRI scan was therefore ordered and revealed a damaged medial cartilage.

Today, the pain was mild but the swelling has not reduced. Mr. Taylor is keen to resolve the issue as it is affecting his ability to work and support his family.

In view of the above, I believe he needs an arthroscopy to remove the damaged cartilage to prevent osteoarthritis in the future.

Yours sincerely

Doctor

INTRODUCTION TO OET SPEAKING SUB-TEST

The test can be segmented into three sessions.

1. ***Warm up session***:   In the beginning, your identity and profession are checked by the interlocutor. Then, he/she will start a conversation about your professional background. This section of the Speaking sub-test is not assessed. You can use this time to familiarize and gain confidence in speaking to the interlocutor.

2 & 3.   **Role-plays 1 & 2** respectively: After the warm up session, you are given two role-plays each with a different scenario, which are introduced one by one. These two role-plays are based on typical workplace situation to demonstrate your ability to deal with situations that occur in the workplace. In each role-play, you take your professional role while the interlocutor may be playing one among the following four roles:
   1.   a patient
   2.   a client
   3.   a patient's relative
   4.   a patient's carer

You will have three minutes to prepare for each. If you have any questions about the content of the role-play or how a role-play works, you can ask them during this preparation time. You can also ask the interlocutor if you have any questions about what a word/phrase means or how it is pronounced. Use the preparation time to think about which elements of the role-play might require you to explain something in more detail or to ask the patient for more clarification.

The role-plays take about five minutes each. It is usual for a role-play to come to a natural end at around the 5-minute mark. If this does not happen, the interlocutor will signal clearly that it is time to conclude the role-play. You will receive information for each role-play on a card that you can keep while you do the role-play. The card will explain the situation and what you are required to do.

You can make notes on the role-play cards if you want, and you can refer to the card at any time during the role-play. However, you must return the card to the interlocutor at the end of the role-play. The interlocutor follows a script so that the speaking test structure is similar for each candidate. The interlocutor also has detailed information to use in each role-play.

Always remember your test day interlocutor plays no role in the assessment of your performance. The whole Speaking test is recorded and it is this audio recording that is assessed. The recorded Speaking sub-test is marked independently by a minimum of two trained OET Assessors. Neither Assessor knows what scores the other has given you, or what scores you have achieved on any of the other sub-tests.

OET Assessors are trained to focus on how a candidate responds to the particular task on the day. They apply specific assessment criteria that reflect the demands of communication in the health professional workplace. (described in the next section). Candidates who are familiar with the assessment criteria and pay attention to the details of the specific role-play task have a better chance of demonstrating their ability in the key areas. Whereas, candidates who use memorized material or merely rely on techniques that worked in other circumstances tend not to perform to their full potential in the test.

You do not have to worry if the interlocutor stops the role-play after five minutes. There is no penalty for not completing all the elements on the role card. However, the more elements of the role-play you cover, the more evidence you are likely to give of your ability to communicate in spoken English.

Total time taken for the test	– *about 20 minutes*
Warm up session	– *about 4 minutes*
Role plays 1 & 2 (each one)	– *3 minutes preparation time (fixed)*
	– *about 5 minutes for role play*

OET SPEAKING ASSESSMENT CRITERIA

Divided into two sets:

1.   *Linguistic Criteria*
2.   *Clinical Communication Criteria*

I. Linguistic Criteria: used to assess English-language skills and again divided into four sets.

A. Intelligibility

This criterion refers to candidate's capacity to make understandable speech. It is assessed by evaluating pronunciation, intonation, stress, rhythm and accent. To get a better score under this criterion, you should

- **pronounce clearly**

- **pitch the voice appropriately without mumbling**

- **stress selectively and use intonation to emphasize the meaning**

- **exhibit a natural rhythm while speaking in English.**

B. Fluency

This criterion refers to the rate and flow of speech. Evidences in the speaking that may reduce your score under this criterion are:

1.   *searching for sentence structures or words*

2.   *beginning with false starts*

3.   *overuse of fillers like yeah, Ok*

4.   *inappropriate repetition of words or phrases*

To get a better score under this criterion, you should

- *at a normal rate that is easily comprehensible*

- *continuously and smoothly with pauses appropriate to the situation.*

C. Appropriateness of Language

This criterion refers to the ability to use and speak English in a tone according to the circumstances and the patient's situation.

To get a better score under this criterion, you should

- ***use simple expressions while describing medical conditions or procedures that a common person can understand***

- ***use a voice tone according to the situation.***

D. Resources of Grammar and Expression

This criterion refers to the spectrum and accuracy that you exhibit in proper use of grammar and vocabulary.

To get a better score under this criterion, you should

- ***have a good range of vocabulary and grammatical expressions***

- ***paraphrase when necessary***

- ***maintain long utterances using proper cohesive devices***

- ***use idioms precisely***

II.   Clinical Communication Criteria: used to assess how you can conduct a professional workplace communication with the interlocutor who may be acting the role of a patient/ a client/ a patient's relative/ a patient's carer. This criterion is again segmented into five more sub-sections with further division for each sub-section.

A. Indicators of relationship building

A1. Initiating the interaction appropriately

You should start the conversation, since you are the medical professional. It involves:

- ***greeting the patient***

- ***introducing yourself***

- ***explain the nature of the interview and if necessary, you can negotiate too.***

A2. Demonstrating an attentive and respectful attitude

You should always demonstrate attentiveness and respect throughout the role-plays.
These can be show by

- ***attending to the patient's comfort***

- ***asking permission and consent to proceed***

- ***being sensitive to potentially embarrassing or distressing matters.***

A3. Demonstrating a non-judgmental approach

To fulfill criterion you should

- **not judge the patient**

- **reassuringly and non-judgmentally accept the patient's perspective**

- **never attempt to prove that the patient views are wrong**

A4. Showing empathy

To fulfill criterion you should

- **understand plight or feelings in interlocutor's cues**

- **show that understanding back in a supportive way**

  - use non-verbal behaviors like silence and appropriate voice tone

  - use verbal cues that shows your understanding of emotions or plight

B. Indicators of understanding & incorporating the patient's perspective

B1. Eliciting and exploring patient's concerns

To fulfill criterion you should **volunteer to take the initiative to elicit and explore unique experience of sickness that interlocutor enact, by probing direct statements or cues conveyed by interlocutor.**

B2. Picking up the patient's cues

For picking up cues, you should use techniques such as:

1. ***Echoing:*** simply repeating the last words of patient to encourage the further contribution of more factual details and feelings

2. ***Directly checking out patient's statements or clues:*** For example: *I sense that you are little uncomfortable about the explanations you have been given.*

B3. Relating explanations to elicited concerns

To fulfill criterion you should **incorporate patient's perspective into explanations as the role-play progress.**

C. Indicators of providing structure

C1. Sequencing the interview logically

To fulfill criterion you should

- **keep a logical sequence as you lead the role play**

- **maintain an ordered approach for both information gathering and giving**

- **also be flexible at any instant to focus on any concerns that patient may present out of the blue**

C2. Signposting changes in topic

To fulfill criterion you should **use words or phrases to express the relation between two ideas within a sentence or two/more sentences to make a smooth transition from one point to the next while speaking.**

For example,
Firstly, ...
Secondly, ...
Similarly, ...

C3. Organizing techniques in explanations

To fulfill criterion you should use organizing techniques such as:

1) **Categorization:** refers to arranging information into categories while you give out information to the patient.

2) **Labeling:** refers to marking the important points using emphatic phrases or adverb intensifiers like definitely, especially, etc., to persuade the patient while giving advice.

3) **Chunking:** refers to delivering a huge piece of information in small pieces by using pauses in between them in order to let the patient understand the points clearly.

D. Indicators for information gathering

D1. Using active listening techniques and avoiding interruptions

To fulfill criterion you should

- **be supportive and show interest during the role play**

- **Pick up cues of the patient's feelings and emotions.**

- **avoid interrupting while the patient is speaking**

D2. Using open questions in the beginning and appropriately moving to closed questions

To fulfill criterion you should

- **use open question in the beginning of exploring of any concern.**

- **use closed questions only when it is necessary to get more specifics from the patient.**

D3. NOT using compound questions or leading questions

To fulfill criterion you should

- ***avoid compound question:*** refers to more than one question, in a single delivery that can confuse the patient. For example, Have you had trouble with sleep or bowel?

- ***avoid leading question***: refers to a question with your assumption in the question itself, which makes it hard for the patient to contradict your assumption. For example, You haven't had any migraines?

D4. Clarifying statements, which are vague,

To fulfill criterion you should ***you may need to prompt patients for more precision, clarity or completeness, when patients' statements can have two (or more) possible meanings and you've to ascertain which one is the intended.***

D5. Summarizing information to encourage correction or to contribute more if information is omitted

To fulfill criterion you should ***take initiative to make the summary of the information gathered so far from the patient and providing an opportunity to the patient to correct if something is different from what you have understood or add if the patient has missed something.***

E. Indicators for information giving

E1. Establishing initially what the patient already knows

To fulfill criterion you should **determine how much and what information the patient needs, and the degree to which your view of the problem differs from that of the patient.**

E2. Periodically pausing and using the response while giving information

To fulfill criterion you should **give information in small pieces by pausing in between and checking for understanding and should be guided by the patient's reactions before proceeding to see what information is required next.**

E3. Encouraging the patient to contribute reactions and feelings

To fulfill criterion you should **provide opportunities to the patient to ask questions, clarifications or doubts.**

E4. Checking whether the patient has understood information

To fulfill criterion you can **either ask plainly whether the patient understood the information being provided or by asking, the patient to repeat back what has been discussed so far to ensure that the patient's understanding is the same as yours.**

E5. Discovering what further information the patient needs

To fulfill criterion you should **ask the patient deliberately about what other information would be helpful to the patient and asking directly is an obvious way to prevent the omission of any important information.**

STRUCTURE OF A ROLE PLAY

A typical role-play can be divided to five parts according to the order of the progress in the interview.

1. Introducing yourself as a healthcare professional to the patient.

_____

2. Finding the 'Chief Concern' from the patient perspective.

3. Gathering all the relevant information from the patient.

4. Giving all the relevant information to the patient and answering additional concerns.

_____

5. Concluding the role-play professionally.

The tasks given for a role-play will be generally based on parts 2, 3 and 4.

Things to Remember

1. You should take the initiative to introduce yourself. Do not wait for the interlocutor to begin the conversation after he informs that your 3 minutes preparation time is over.

2. Don't start giving out information (part 4) before fulfilling part 2 and 3.

3. Don't conclude before confirming whether patient understood all the information that you provided.

Introducing Yourself As A Healthcare Professional

Examples:

Hello. My name is Sarah Delaware and I am

> */the medical practitioner, on the team that will be looking after you.*

> */ the orthopedic surgeon who will be performing your hip replacement.*

> */ one of the ward doctors on duty this afternoon.*

>> */Can you give me your name, please?*

>> */ May I know your name please?*

Or if the name is given in the role play card

Hello Simon,

> */you are here regarding your blood test results are not you?*

> */how are you feeling today?*

> */you are looking better today. How do you feel?*

> */what has brought you along here today?*

> */Why have you come to see me today?*

2. Finding the 'Chief Concern' from the patient perspective.

Mr/Mrs. Martin, (what brings/ what concerns bring you here today?) / (what would you like to discuss?)/ (can you tell me what you are concerned/worried about?)/ (Can you tell me what you have difficulty/ problems with?)

3. Gathering all the relevant information from the patient.

Now, you should listen attentively. Listen to the patient's answer without interrupting or efficiently make use of continuers like – *Mm-hmm /Uh-hmm / Uh huh /Go on/ I see/ Right,* to maintain the flow of the patient's conversation. When the patient finish his/her story ask again if there is something more to it. Use open-ended questions like:

Is there something else?

Open & Closed Questions

Open questions: encourage the patient to give more information and explain more about their emotions and behaviors. These questions require more than a yes/ no/ a short answer and often begin with question words like what, how, or tell me. They do not require a precise answer, so the patient is free to talk anything about the question.

For example:

Tell me more about the accident.

Closed questions: are used for finding specific information. They are often yes or no questions or questions that are to be answered in a few words. Overuse of such questions can end up in incomplete responses by discouraging a complete disclosure from the patient. Therefore, they are only efficient, when it comes to collect specific information needed during the OET role-play.

For example:

Does this answer your question?

4.   *Giving all the relevant information to the patient and answering additional concerns.*

The general relationship between common concerns and their respective information to be given according to the tasks mentioned in the role-play card are like:

- In case of diabetes, it will be to minimize the sugar and carbohydrate rich food intake.

- In case of hypertension, it will be to minimize high-fat and high-salt content food intake.

- In case of lung problems, it will be to quit smoking.

- In case of liver problems, it will be to quit drinking.

Therefore, you have to provide the relevant information in such a way that it is not criticizing the patient.

For example:

I am afraid your weight/smoking/alcohol consumption/intake can worsen/deteriorate your condition.

Reducing your weight/smoking/alcohol consumption/intake is an essential step towards avoiding medical problems like heart diseases.

I do understand your reluctance. It is a daunting prospect to make such huge changes in your everyday routine. However, you must consider the risks associated with smoking/ drinking/ carrying excess weight.

Informing the patient

Based on my examination it will be necessary to...

The x-ray indicates that your child has...

The blood test results indicate that child has...

The tests show that it is probably a condition known as...

Describing the condition

Make sure your explanation is clear and well organized.

For example:

The blood tests results indicate that you have Hepatitis A. Do you know anything about this condition? (No) Okay I will explain it to you. It is a condition caused by.... The symptoms include... The best treatment is to... It is highly contagious so you need to....

Try not to talk continuously. Stop from time to time to check if the patient understands your explanation.

Is that clear?

Do you understand so far?

Do you have any questions?

Reassuring the patient

Commonly, the patient will be concerned about their condition or treatment method, so there are some standard expressions you can use to reassure the patient.

It is nothing to get alarmed about. It is just a routine check.

There really is nothing to worry about. It is a standard procedure.

Let me reassure you, if you follow my advice, the risks of future problems will be greatly reduced.

Persuading the patient

If you return to work, you run the risk of doing further damage to your health.

What is more important? The risk of permanent damage to your arm or a single game?

Let me reassure you, if you follow my advice, the risk of heart attack will be greatly reduced. However if you do not follow my advice, and continue to smoke and drink heavily, then the risk of heart attack is much higher.

In some other cases, you have to negotiate a plan with the patient according to the tasks given and in such cases begin with starters like:

Here is what I propose we do. [plan in your own words].

Given your health, a better solution might be [plan in your own words].

If you are willing to accept a compromise, how about [plan in your own words]?

You would also have to answer any additional concerns that the patient might bring up while you giving information with patience.

5. Concluding the role-play professionally.

Between now and then/next visit if you have any problem do not hesitate to come and see me.

Well, if you run into any problems, I want you to call and come to see me. Just to see how you are coming along. So, make an appointment and I will see you then.

If there is any concluding tasks in the role play card like, scheduling an appointment for review or offer a patient information-leaflet, you can conclude the role-play right after fulfilling the task. For example:

Thank you, for all the information you have given me. Here is a patient – information leaflet that you will find useful. If you have any additional questions, please, do not hesitate to contact me.

If there are any concluding tasks in the role-play card, you can directly guide the conversation to a proper closing. For example:

Well, it was great meeting you. Please, call the hospital if you have any questions. Our number is on your label.

At a suburban medical clinic or general practice

Please make an appointment with reception to see me in a week. Take care now.

Here is your prescription. Take it to your chemist and they will give you the medication. All the best.

Thanks for coming to see me today.

Please come and see me again in a week.

I would like to see your child again in two months time. Take care now.

In a hospital ward

I will come back and check on your condition later today.

If there is any change in your condition please let me know.

If you need me again, just press the buzzer.

HOW TO IMPROVE YOUR OET SPEAKING SKILLS

To improve your OET speaking skills, you can develop the required skills by working through the following stages.

Stage 1

- Write out dialogues of a medical interview between a health professional and patient using the role-play scenarios.

- Research medical conditions and learn how to explain them simply and clearly in nonprofessional (common person)'s language.

- Practice doing the role-plays at home by yourself or even better with a friend and record your voice.

- Analyze your own speaking and keep practicing until your fluency, range of expression, grammar and confidence improves. Ask yourself the following questions:

-

   ✓   *Could I ask appropriate questions?*

   ✓   *Was able to clearly explain the dental condition?*

   ✓   *Was my fluency good?*

   ✓   *Did I hesitate a lot?*

   ✓   *Was my pronunciation clear?*

   ✓   *Was my grammar and sentence structure accurate?*

✓ *Could I lead the role-play?*

- *Do this every day with different conditions and keep doing it until you feel confident in your ability to complete a medical interview.*

Stage 2

Once you have developed confidence and have a good understanding of how to structure a medical interview you can begin doing role-plays by simply researching the topic, but not reading the role-play cards. This will give you a good idea of your level, and your ability to respond appropriately to the patient without preparation. Make sure you continue to record your own speech, so that can identify your strengths and weaknesses and do the necessary study.

Stage 3

The final stage is when you can confidently respond to any role- play scenario, regardless of the topic, and complete a medical interview without any preparation, apart from the 3 minutes allowed by OET on exam day. Once you have reached this stage, you will know you have a chance of achieving a B grade or higher.

Dos

- Do always maintain an audibly pleasant pitch.

- Do control intonation by rising or falling the voice to enhance the meaning

- Do alternate between stressed and unstressed syllables.

- Do take pauses between phrases.

- Do use appropriate synonyms.

- Do connect phrases into lengthy utterances.

- Do use varying transitional words.

- Do use medical idioms according to the situation.

- Do read the role-play card carefully and ask the interlocutor if you are unsure of any of the words or expressions in the task.

- Do react to what the interlocutor (as patient) asks or says and respond accordingly. This is much more important than simply following the tasks on the card.

- Do focus on the patient and respond to their questions and concerns.

- Do take charge of the role-play. You are a medical professional and should act accordingly by leading the role-play. This means you must start and conclude the role-play, and if the patient is quite or silent, then it is your responsibility to keep the conversation moving.

- Do utilize the allowed 2~3 minutes to identify the key points on your card including:
  - the setting
  - whether you know the patient, or if it's the first time to meet
  - the main topic of conversation and relevant background information
  - task requirements

- Do refer to your card occasionally during the exam, especially if you are unsure of what to say.

- Do be prepared to discuss matters, which are not on your card. The patient's card usually contains information, which is not on your card.

- Do look at the patient during the role-play. Although only your speech is recorded, your communication will be more effective if you have eye contact with the interviewer.

- Do stay focused on the task at hand. You only have 5 minutes to complete all the tasks!

- Do practice as many tasks as possible with a partner to ensure you are familiar with the speaking test. Remember it is very different to IELTS and requires different language skills, such as the ability to persuade, convince and reassure.

- Do act confidently and speak with a positive voice. If you are unsure of the details of the condition, it is okay to make it up! Remember it is a test of English not your medical knowledge.

- Do slow down your speech when using unfamiliar words such as names of medications or treatment procedures. Always be prepared to explain the meaning of any medical terminology you use.

- Do regularly check that the patient understands your explanations. Ask questions such as:
  Is that clear?

- Do stop speaking if the patient wants to interrupt you. You must respond to the patient.

- Correct a grammatical or vocabulary mistake immediately if you are aware that you have made one.

- Do be aware of the gender of your patient and if you say he instead of she, try to correct it.

Don'ts

- Do not create your own idioms/translate idioms from other languages.

- Do not omit relevant information while paraphrasing.

- Do not speak with words that are hard to grasp for listener.

- Do not speak with wrong grammatical structures.

- Do not utter complex terms for medical conditions or procedures.

- Do not stress on the wrong syllable.

- Do not speak without intonation.

- Do not show the influence of mother tongue while English speaking.

- Do not try to fake an accent or use mixed accents.

- Do not plan what you are going to say in advance. React to the scenario on your role-play card and plan your role accordingly.

- Do not plan what you are going to say in advance. React to the scenario on your role-play card and plan your role accordingly.

- Do not be card focused at the expense of the patient. It is much more important to respond to the patient in a natural and caring manner (where required).

- Do not wait for the interviewer to lead the role-play. They may not and this is your job.

- Do not rush through your card in 30 seconds and say you are ready to start! You may miss some important details.

- Do not try to memorize the whole card. You can refer to it as required during the role-play.

- Do not feel you must complete every aspect of your task. Remember it is a guide only and you will not be penalized, if you do not complete every detail of your card.

- Don't look at you card only and read it while the patient is talking as you must listen carefully to what they the patient says so that you can respond appropriately.

- Do not spend too much time on unrelated matters such as a detailed medical history as you do not have time for this.

- Do not ignore the task requirements and say what you think based on your medical knowledge. Remember it is a test of English language ability and not a place to demonstrate your medical knowledge.

- Do not show how nervous you are. This can negatively affect your result. Lots of practice is the best way to overcome nerves.

- Do not use a lot of medical jargon and technical words. You need to use nonprofessional's language to describe the condition.

- Do not speak in a continuously in a monologue. You are taking part in a 2-way conversation.

- Do not talk over the patient.

- Do not rush your sentences, as you are more likely to make an error. Try to remain calm and in control.

MISCELLANEOUS QUESTIONS

How old are you?

Are you married?

Do you have any children?

Do you have a partner?

How frequently do you have sex?

When did you last have sex?

Do you use any form of contraception?

Have you had any serious problem in the past?

Have you ever been in hospital for any reason?

Have you had any problem with pregnancy?

Have you ever had accident or injuries?

Have you ever had problem with your pregnancy?

Have you ever had accidents or injuries?

Is there anything else I need to know?

What do you think your problem is?

How do you think I can help you?

When did you first have the problem?

What do you understand by 'heartburn'?

When have you been getting it?

Have you ever noticed any particular kind of other discomfort, perhaps associated with the heartburn?

Do any particular foods seem to bring on your heartburn?

Now, have you noticed that any particular foods that trigger the heartburn?

Family history

Is anyone taking regular medication?

How old was your father when he died?

Does anybody in your family have serious illness?

When did you last go abroad and where?

Drug history

Are you taking any medication now?

Did you take it regularly on time?

To what extent, was it successful?

Do you use any over-counter remedies/ herbal/ homeopathy?

Do you know if you allergic to drug?

Past history

Have you ever fainted?

Have you ever had any dizziness?

Do you get ringing in your ears?

Have you ever had any numbness in your limbs?

Weight

What is your weight?

How much do you weight?

As you know, your weight is not proportional to your height. You need to lose your weight.

You should cut down on your smoking / your fatty foods.

Work

What are your work hours like?

Do you have work at the weekend?

Do you have to stand around (per day) a lot, on your work?

Do you work shift / on shift?

What did you do before this job?

How long have you been out of job?

How long were you in that job?

Alcohol

What about alcohol?

What do you normally drink?

How much do you drink in the week?

How often do you drink?

What is the most you would drink in a week?

Can you give up alcohol if you want?

Are you aware of any difference in your alcohol consumption over the past few years?

Pregnancy

How long did your pregnancy last?

Did you have any trouble during your pregnancy, such as high blood pressure?

How long were you in labor?

Have you had a miscarriage?

Menstrual problems

Are your periods regular?

How often do you get them?

When was your last period?

How old were you when you start to get them?

How long do your periods usually last?

Would you say they are light or heavy?

Do you feel edgy (nervous condition) or irritable?

Do you get clot?

How many pads do you use each day?

Have you seen clot?

Do you get period pains?

Have you had any discharge?

What color is it?

Do the flushes interrupt your sleep?

When did you see the last one?

Did it come on slowly or suddenly?

Does it wake you up at night?

What type of pain do you have?

Have they made you feel sick?

Stress

Are you worried?

What sort of things make you stressed?

What do you do to relieve it?

Are you worried about anything?

Baby problem

Do you give him foods supplement (supplementary foods)?

What is his appetite like?

Is he breast-fed or bottle-fed?

Do you eat low fat dairy product?

I am afraid calorie is necessary for the child growth.

The more calories you give him, his growth will be better.

Difficult patient

I cannot find anything seriously wrong with you. Nevertheless, I would like to have some blood tests before you leave the hospital.

That really interests me.

Tell me more.

It seems important.

Tell me more about things at home/work.

Are you afraid that something bad is going to happen to you?

Is your relationship with any particular person causing you stress?

I am concern about what you are not telling me.

What kind of troubles have you been having?

... Yes, I understand please continue.

Ok, we will come to that later/ we will deal with that later.

However, I hope the problem will solve with this medications.

Confrontation

You look sad.

You seem frightened.

You sound angry.

You seem tense.

You seem very sad today.

It seems your having trouble coping.

You seem to be telling me that.

Is there anything else I can help you?

Summarizing

If I have understood you correctly, you have told me …. If there are any questions, I will be pleased to answer them.

Physical exam

I am going to press gently on your stomach, let me to know if you feel pain. Well, I will check you out, then after that, we will talk.

I will just take your blood pressure now. Would you roll up your sleeve, please?

Could you slip into this gown and leave it open at the back. I am going to check your pulse.

Giving Advice

If you want to get rid of the infection, you will need to persevere. You will need to complete the course, to allow them to take effect. I am afraid only antibiotic will clear this up.

The less you smoke, the sooner you will recover.

With all due respect to your doctor, but I am not agreeing with him. It might not very delicious, but it is healthier.

ESSENTIAL VERBS IN ROLE PLAY

Start	*Decline*	*Assure*
Come on	*Lower*	*Inflammate*
Bring on	*Weaken*	*Swell*
Break out	*Strengthen*	*Protrude*
Notice	*Increase*	*Appear*
Seem	*Raise*	*Disappear*
Sound	*Recover*	*Get infected*
Experience	*Get rid of*	*Feel*
Get	*Feel better*	*Suffer from*
Get used to	*Clear up*	*Bother*
Have got	*Improve*	*Take care*
Transmit	*Prescribe*	*Watch (your weight)*
Trigger	*Apply (cream)*	*Consider*
Trigger off	*Perhaps*	*Control*
Stimulate	*Suppose*	*Help*
Aggravate	*Insist*	*Manipulate*
Provoke	*Recommend*	*Cut down (on)*

Deteriorate	Advise	Cut off
Worsen	Refer	Quit
Sort out	Check	Keep away
Sooth	Explain	Be aware of
Alleviate	Arrange	Be complaining of
Alley	Make	Reduce
Relieve	Promise	Persevere

OET SPEAKING SUB-TEST SAMPLE QUESTIONS

NOTE: There are no sample answers for these questions as it may limit your scope of the conversation that can happen in the real test.

OET SAMPLE TEST 1

ROLE PLAYER CARD NO. 1	MEDICINE

SETTING	Operating Theatre Suite
PATIENT	You are 45 years old. You are waiting for a day procedure to have a large lump removed from your back. The lump is about 10 cm in diameter and you find it unsightly. You are also concerned that it may be cancerous. Your GP has assured you that it is a benign lipoma, not a cancer, but you remain unconvinced. The surgeon has already seen you to confirm your consent for the procedure but you have some further questions. You have asked for a doctor to talk to you.
TASK	

- Explain your worry that the lump is cancerous. Ask how the surgeon will know whether it is or not.

- You have been told to come back to the outpatient clinic in two weeks. Find out why it takes so long for the results. Will you learn then if the lump was cancerous?

- Express concern about the possibility of a scar on your back. What can you do to minimize this?

- Ask about the chance of the lump returning or a similar lump growing elsewhere on your body. What if the surgeon doesn't remove it all? You are very anxious.

OET SAMPLE TEST 1	
CANDIDATE CARD NO. 1	**MEDICINE**

SETTING	Operating Theatre Suite
DOCTOR	You are working as a surgical resident in this hospital. You have been called to talk to a 45-year-old patient who is awaiting surgery for a large benign lipoma on his/her back. You note that the patient has already been booked into the outpatient clinic in two weeks for review of the wound and histopathology.
TASK	

- Reassure the patient that the risk of cancer is extremely low.

- Explain that the lump will be examined under the microscope and the patient will normally get the results at the two-week review in the clinic. The wound will also be checked then.

- Explain that there will be a scar as it is a large lesion but it will fade with time. Keeping the area dressed with steristrips for a month can help to minimize this. The surgeon will discuss this further with the patient.

- Reassure the patient about removal of the lump and the unlikelihood of recurrence.

OET SAMPLE TEST 2	
ROLE PLAYER CARD NO. 1	**MEDICINE**

SETTING	Hospital
PATIENT	You are 52 years old and have been admitted 10 hospitals with diverticulitis. Your doctor thinks it will settle down within one week with some antibiotics. As a highly anxious person, you are concerned that you may have bowel cancer because your mother died of bowel cancer.
TASK	• Seek confirmation that you really have diverticulitis, as you have never heard of it.
	• Explain your family history of bowel cancer (mother died of bowel cancer at 55 years old).
	• Ask what you can do to prevent the same fate for yourself. You spend a lot of time worrying about this.
	• Accept the doctor's advice and reassurance that you are doing everything possible to Identify any bowel changes early (e.g., good diet, awareness of signs and symptoms, regular check-ups, colonoscopy).

OET SAMPLE TEST 2	
CANDIDATE CARD NO. 1	**MEDICINE**

SETTING	Hospital
DOCTOR	Your 52-year old patient has been admitted to hospital with diverticulitis. You think it will settle down within one week with some antibiotics. Your patient Is a highly anxious person and is concerned that he/she may have bowel cancer because his/her mother died of bowel cancer.
TASK	

- Confirm the diagnosis (CT scan) of diverticulitis.

- Explain diverticulitis (inflammation of the diverticula, which are out pockets of the bowel mucosa).

- Find out about the patient's family history and explain that family history of bowel cancer is important but prevention and early detection for all people is highly advisable.

- Reassure the patient that he/she is doing everything possible to identify any changes that could lead to early detection of cancer (e.g. good diet. awareness of signs and symptoms, regular check-ups, colonoscopy when indicated).

- Explain the need to avoid constipation and to maintain a high fiber diet and soft stool consistency.

OET SAMPLE TEST 3	
ROLE PLAYER CARD NO. 1	**MEDICINE**

SETTING	Suburban General Practice
PATIENT	You are a 23-year-old student. You have been feeling more tired than usual over the past few months since you started studying for exams. You feel stressed and have had difficulty getting to sleep at night. You have no other symptoms. You have a good diet and do not drink or smoke, but you do not do any exercise. Last week the doctor examined you and ordered some blood tests. You are here for the results. You have an exam in two weeks and want a medical certificate to say you are too sick to sit it.
TASK	

- Ask about the results of your blood tests.

- Find out why you are feeling tired.

- Ask for a medical certificate for your exam, which is in two weeks' time.

- Become stressed and anxious when the doctor will not write you a certificate, and express your concern that you will fail the exam.

- Try to get the doctor to feel sorry for you (exams have a terrible effect on you).

- Finally agree to try what the doctor recommends and to see him/her again in the week before the exams.

OET SAMPLE TEST 3

CANDIDATE CARD NO. 1	MEDICINE

SETTING	Suburban General Practice
DOCTOR	This 23-year-old student presented a week ago complaining of tiredness. He/she described difficulty getting to sleep and stress over upcoming exams. He/ she has had no other symptoms and is not clinically depressed. Examination last week was completely normal. You ordered some basic blood tests and the results are all normal.
TASK	

- Reassure the patient that there is no major medical cause for his/her symptoms.

- Explain that stresses from exams and poor sleep are the likely causes of the symptoms.

- Suggest regular gentle exercise and avoidance of stimulants like coffee and sugary foods; encourage him/her to find time to relax.

- Explain that you cannot write a medical certificate for a time in the future.

- Find out about his/her concerns about exams and respond sympathetically.

- Suggest that he/she try your recommendations and come back next week so you can review how he/she is getting on.

OET SAMPLE TEST 4	
ROLE PLAYER CARD NO. 1	**MEDICINE**

SETTING	Community Health Centre
PATIENT	You are 25 years old, salesperson. You have an outbreak of ulcers on your tongue, which started last night. You have suffered from these on and off since, you were a child, including several attacks in recent months. Usually they clear up after a few days. Six months ago, you started working as a salesperson. It is a high-pressure job. You need to talk a Jot and often entertain clients. The mouth ulcers really bother you when speaking, eating or drinking. You feel irritable with them and you are worried that your work is being affected. You are generally well.
TASK	

- Answer the doctor's questions about your general health.

- Ask for something to clear up your ulcers within 24 hours (you have to speak at an important meeting tomorrow).

- Insist on something more effective than antiseptic gel from the pharmacy – it never helps much.

- Try to find out what causes the the ulcers, how to stop them from recurring.

OET SAMPLE TEST 4	
CANDIDATE CARD NO. 1	**MEDICINE**

SETTING	Community Health Centre
DOCTOR	The patient is a 25 years old salesperson, who presents with tiny, off-white ulcers on the tongue. On examination, the patient clearly has good dental hygiene.
TASK	

- Question the patient to exclude diabetes mellitus and inflammatory bowel disease as underlying conditions, and herpes simplex as a cause (fever symptoms?).

- You suspect aphthous ulcers (no known cause. but some research suggests an immune reaction - could be related to stress, hormones, virus or allergy).

- Recommend a blood test to check for infection.

- Discuss management of the symptoms (rinse with warm, salty water or medicated mouthwash, apply antiseptic gel, take paracetamol, have plenty of fluids, avoid spicy and sour foods).

- The ulcers will resolve by themselves in a few days.

- Offer to prescribe an anti-inflammatory drug if pain persists.

- Advise the patient on a healthy lifestyle.

OET SAMPLE TEST 5

ROLE PLAYER CARD NO. 1	MEDICINE

SETTING	Suburban Clinic
PATIENT	You are middle-aged and overweight. You have noticed a bitter taste in your mouth, which is worse on waking in the morning and is accompanied by a burning sensation in the back of the throat. You have also noticed it is worse during your morning walk after breakfast. Sometimes there is a bit of regurgitation of food. You smoke 5-10 cigarettes a day. Drink several cups of coffee, and have two glasses of wine with dinner. You also have a slight cough when you speak.
TASK	

- Find out what is causing these symptoms.

- When the doctor mentions reflux, become alarmed. You have heard that it can lead to a serious pre-cancerous condition.

- Find out how it can be treated.

- Do not accept the doctor's recommendation. You feel he/she is not taking this seriously enough and you want to see a specialist. Be insistent.

- Reluctantly accept the doctor's advice.

OET SAMPLE TEST 5	
CANDIDATE CARD NO. 1	**MEDICINE**

SETTING	Suburban Clinic
DOCTOR	A middle-aged patient has come in complaining of a bitter taste in his/her mouth, which is worse on waking and accompanied by a burning sensation in the back of the throat. He/she is overweight, and you notice a slight cough when he/she speaks. You diagnose GORD (gastro-esophageal reflux disease).
TASK	

- Check if the patient has difficulty swallowing.

- Tell the patient your diagnosis (GORD) and explain the causes {e.g., alcohol use, being overweight. smoking, bad posture).

- Outline dietary and lifestyle measures that can help in controlling it (e.g., weight management - foods to avoid; meals - little and often and not within three hours of bed; lifestyle - smoking, alcohol, elevation of head of bed, avoidance of exercise straight after meal).

- Advise on the treatment strategy: ranitidine (H2 antagonist) then review.

- Reassure the patient. You do not feel a referral for an endoscopy is warranted at this stage. It may be worthwhile later if there is limited response to ranitidine

INTRODUCTION TO OET LISTENING SUB-TEST

The Listening sub-test is designed to assess a range of listening skills, such as identifying specific information, detail, gist, opinion or the speaker's purpose. These skills are assessed through note-completion tasks and multiple-choice questions. The Listening sub-test is divided into 3 parts, and 42 questions. Across all three parts, a range of accents is used to reflect the global nature of the healthcare workforce. The main accents are Australian, British, American, and other varieties such as New Zealand, Irish, Canadian, South Africa, etc.

The topics will be of generic healthcare interest, which is accessible to candidates across all professions. Therefore, the health professionals in a listening extract may be any one of the 12 professions who can take OET. The total length of the Listening sub-test is 50 minutes and the Listening audio is about 40 minutes, including recorded speech and pauses to allow you time to write your answers. You will hear each recording once only and are expected to write your answers while you are listening. You will have two minutes at the end of the sub-test to check your answers for all three parts of the sub-test. The test-takers usually award grade B to the candidates, who have a score of at least 30 marks.

You can use abbreviations that are commonly accepted in your profession and which are clear to other professionals, for example "BP" for blood pressure. However, you should avoid abbreviations that are specific to a particular workplace or specialism, because these might not be commonly understood. OET assessors are trained to accept a reasonable range of abbreviations, but OET does not refer to any specific dictionaries or lists.

There is no penalty for including information that is not in the marking guide. However, you will lose marks if you contradict yourself or make your meaning unclear. Names for conditions and medications are often difficult to spell, therefore in the Listening sub-test; you will not be penalized for misspelling, provided the meaning is clear to other healthcare professionals. Any reasonable attempt at spelling the correct answer has a good chance of being accepted. Where possible, reference is made in the audio recording to both the generic and brand names for medications, and to both medical and lay terms discussed during the consultations. The marking guide gives assessors extensive guidance on the range of misspellings, which are to be accepted.

Please note that the Listening sub-test is different from the Reading and Writing sub-tests in the way misspellings are treated. Therefore, do not waste time hanging around for the correct spelling of names for conditions and medications that are often difficult to spell.

OET LISTENING SUB-TEST STRUCTURE

Part A (24 marks)

Part A consists of two consultation-recorded extracts to assess your ability to identify specific information during a consultation. You will listen to two recorded health professional-patient consultations for about 5 minutes each and you will complete the health professional's notes using the information you hear. In Part A, you must complete the notes using the same words you hear on the recording. You should not paraphrase the information and you should not change the information.

Your answers for Part A are double-marked by trained OET assessors. These answers are randomly assigned to assessors to avoid any conflict of interest. For Part A, you must write your answers in the space provided in the question booklet.

Part A is all about gathering specific information, usually from what the patient says. You do not have to waste time making sure your grammar is perfect. Often, grammar words like articles are given in the answer key itself. OET Assessors are specifically instructed to accept small grammatical and spelling errors.

In Part A you have to write down information as note completion; so, carefully listen for words, which indicate the structure of what the speaker is saying. This includes names or terms, which match headings on the page. These will help guide you through the information on the page and choose answers, which fit logically.

In Part A, write your answers directly onto the lines provided for the two extracts in the question booklet. The length of the line should be sufficient to write the correct answer.

Part B (6 marks)

Part B consists of six short workplace recorded extracts (e.g. team briefings, handovers, or health professional-patient dialogues) of about 1 minute each to assess your ability to identify the purpose of short extracts from the healthcare workplace. You will have to answer one multiple-choice question for each extract you hear.

Part B is more about understanding the main idea of the communication between two healthcare colleagues, a healthcare professional and their patient or by a healthcare professional to a group of colleagues. You have to choose the most relevant option from the given three, which represents the content of the communication. All the answer options may be offered; therefore, it is always important to check which one is covered completely.

Part C (12 marks)

Part C consists of two presentation extracts of about 5 minutes each to assess your ability to follow a recorded presentation or interview on a range of accessible healthcare topics. You will have to answer six multiple-choice questions for each extract.

Part C contains two main types of listening questions; (1) understanding direct meaning and (2) understanding inferred meaning. In questions about direct meaning, you will for instance be asked about the speaker's main idea. In questions about inferred meaning might focus on the speaker's attitude. As it is in Part B, you need to choose the most relevant option from the given three to answer each question. The difference is that In Part C you have to demonstrate deeper understanding of the meaning of what has been said rather than the main idea.

Note: In multiple-choice tasks (Part B and Part C), be careful not to choose an option just because you hear a word or phrase from it on the recording. Think about the whole meaning of what is said and match it to the closest option.

Your answers for Part B and Part C are computer scanned and automatically scored; therefore, it is essential that you follow the instructions provided on the front page of the question booklet when entering your answers. You must fill in the circle containing your chosen answer A, B or C using a 2B pencil. Working as quickly as you can, shade in the whole of the circle including the letter with your pencil so it can be clearly read by the computer. If you want to change your answer, erase it and fill in the circle of the answer you now want to choose. Answers written elsewhere in your booklet will not be marked.

Tips To Improve Your Listening Sub-Test Performance

1) Developing your Listening skills

You should broaden your ability to deal with fresh content and unfamiliar voices by listening to radio programs and online lectures; never limit your listening practice to test preparation materials. Listening skills can be developed by listening regularly to a wide range of speech, at natural speeds, from speakers with different accents in different healthcare contexts. Try to listen to sources where the speaker is giving their own point of view. This will give you a proper practice in identifying and following the speaker's line of argument and attitude, which is very different from picking out factual content.

2) Using the pauses efficiently

For all parts of the test, use the pauses included in the recording to read the question booklet carefully; this will help you identify what you need to listen for. Remember that your main objective is to answer correctly; it may not be necessary to understand every word you hear.

3) Managing your time efficiently

In the Listening sub-test, you hear the recording only once, so it is very important to write your answers as you listen. You check your answers during the short breaks between each question or at the 2-minute period in the end of the sub-test. Use this time to check that you have clearly answered each question and written your answers for Part A legibly.

OET LISTENING STRATEGIES

Question Type Specific Listening Strategies

<u>*Sentence Completion Questions*</u> *(in part A)*

In this type of questions, it is important to look at the question before the speaker starts speaking and identify the key word in the question. It will prepare you to listen for the correct answer.

For example:

- *is unhappy at the care home because of* _____

    The 'because of' in the question is obviously asking for a reason, and 'because of' usually needs a noun in the answer. This guess will help you to look specifically for a certain reason with a noun.

    Therefore, when the recording starts, scan the heading above the questions so you will have an idea about what you are going to listen.

    Use your prediction skills wisely– e.g., what vocabulary is likely to come up given this topic. (In this example, the answer is definitely coming from patient's mouth. So, listen carefully for the negative terms like synonyms of unhappy like feel bad or sad, distressed, irritated, not pleased, miserable, pity... etc)

<u>*Multiple Choice Questions*</u> *(in part B & C)*

In this type of questions, you have to look at the question and options carefully to pick out the key words. You should then think of any synonyms or paraphrases that could be used, in both the question and answers provided.

For example:

- *One drawback of exercise ECGs is that they are_____.*

A. *prohibitively expensive*

B. *lacking in precision*

C. *less effective with males*

In the question the keywords are drawback, prohibitively, precision and less effective. You need to think of other ways to say these words, like disadvantage or problem for 'drawback'.

This guess will help you to flag the instances where these key words pop up, and choose which option has the most relevant information according to the question based on your understanding of the content.

General Listening Strategies

- Have a spare pen or pencil ready just in case

- Fill in the cover page correctly

- Stay relaxed and receptive – ready to listen

- Focus on listening and understanding then recording your answer

- Don't try to write everything the speakers say – it is not dictation or a memory test

- Don't be distracted by what is going on around you (e.g., sneezing, a nervous candidate at the next desk)

- Don't lose your place during the test; remain focused on each question

- Use only the common abbreviations that you hear in the listening extract

- Write clearly; don't make it difficult for the assessor to read your responses as you may not get all the marks you could

- Keep looking ahead at what is coming up

- Use the pauses in the recordings to finish writing, review, and prepare for the next section

- Make sure your notes communicate what you intend

- Do not waste valuable time using an eraser to correct a mistake if you make one. Simply cross out any words you don't want the person marking your paper to accept; this takes a lot less time and you will not be penalized

- Think twice about going back to change something – it may be better to leave what you wrote the first time if you are not sure

- Don't leave any blanks; have a guess at the answer

- Check the format of each question: e.g., sentence completion or multiple-choice questions.

- Look for any simple spelling errors that may accidentally change the meaning of your answer ('message' for 'massage', 'bills' for 'pills', etc.).

- Practice, Practice, Practice! This is the most important aspect of improving your ability to take notes. The more you practice the better you will able to take notes and listen at the same time.

- Build your vocabulary. When you encounter new words, find out the meaning and write them down in a vocabulary booklet.

WEBSITE LINKS TO LISTENING EXTRACTS FOR PRACTICE

There are resources on the web, which can help candidates develop the general listening skills involved in a medical context especially on YouTube. You can also check the language style, appropriate use of the language and some medical terms used in the following websites.

ABC Australia Health

- http://www.abc.net.au/health/
  (Health Matters)

- http://www.abc.net.au/rn/allinthemind/
  (All in the Mind)

- http://www.abc.net.au/rn/healthreport/
  (Health Report)

- http://www.abc.net.au/rn/lifematters/
  (Life Matters)

- http://www.abc.net.au/health/minutes/
  (Health Minutes)

BBC World Service Health

- http://www.bbc.co.uk/worldservice/programmes/health_check.shtml
  (Health Check)

-

http://www.bbc.co.uk/worldservice/programmes/science_in_action.shtml
(Science in Action)

Newsletters

You could subscribe to the regular health-related newsletters:

- http://www.abc.net.au/health/subscribe/default.htm

- http://www.englishmed.com/

Made in United States
Orlando, FL
03 September 2022

21951208R00076